EMBRACING NEW LIFE WITH A VIEW

A Praise in Prose

Rachel Cherry Adams

Contents

The Prologue

Some of this book of Prose Poetry is based on the Author's secret journal. Some of these writings were written during some of the most difficult periods - and, of course, the "smooth sailing" as remembered.

Glory, Glory to His Name

Giving Glory to You, Creator of the Universe.

You were there all along from the beginning.

Praising You for Your strength, courage, wisdom, and knowledge to write these pages.

Everything you have given, I'm giving all my best back to You, Almighty One.

As I take inventory of my life, there have been some great hurts, along with an abundance of chuckles to remember alongside the enduring weeping. Through it all, I have been filled with your love, tranquility, and power.

You are so gracious that You even sent some precious angels to keep me level here on earth's ground.

To "the Lifter of My Head", let Thy blessings continue to fall, especially on the people who read this, your book, as Your divine instrument envisioned.

My Sweet Blyss

[A little girl running up to her friend, and then running and looking back as if pretending to hide]

Loving our playtime together.

Entering the room, you squeal at the top of your lungs then run and hide.

It's sort of a hide-and-seek game we got going on between us.

You 2, me at 63.

Complete jovial moments in time spent.

Our own little piece of heaven on this side of grace.

Shine on Bliss,

With that smile and twinkle in your eye!

Everything about you resonates with Heaven.

Ode to the Underdogs

The Underdogs,

Increasingly bringing up the rear.

Please do not misjudge the underdogs,

Sneaking up on you when you are not looking

Underdogs may be slow, and almost last — There are no limitations to the craftiness of these Underdogs.

A Blessed Gift, with the courage to face the universe.

Underdogs are long shots, misunderstood at the finishing line, like in the fable "The Tortoise and the Hare", a reminder that the race is not always to the swift, and there is more to life than increasing its speed.

Keeping at it and sticking it out, is their stead.

Plod on!

Jazee

Love that swing in your sound,

Those riffs in the voice,

High notes, low notes,

We want to dance in jubilation.

What is it about you Jazee that makes us fall in love with you?

Is it the bebop?

Is it the smooth in you?

Thinking about you Jazee, makes one strike out in a "shimmy".

Ode to Jazz.

Speak to Me!

Be changed for good.

This "Little Voice" talks to me right here on earth.

It's not a loud boisterous sound; it's a small whisper that speaks to the heart and mind

When I hear it, I must move!...

> Be in tune with it.

> Recognize what it is.

What about you? Can you hear it?

> Close your eyes, turn off all noises around, for as long as it takes —to connect to this small phenomenal "Voice" of the soul's walking in the faith journey.

Venturing Through this Ebb of Life

Even in this time of shutdown in our world, we can find strength through this trial we call "Coronavirus".

You may ask, "How can we do that?"

Can you hear the faint singing in the distance just before the morning dew appears as the sun is rising on the horizon?

Well! Look at the sunshine when it passes through the windowpane.

> Can you feel the warmness on your skin so warm to the touch? — Not much now, just a dab will do ya.

Look up at the sky, whether it is clear or cloudy, then look out at the backdrop of the trees. —Isn't that a magnificent vision to behold?

Perhaps, it's raining.

> Can't you hear the drops? —If you walk under those drops, can you feel the refreshing spirit of the atmosphere?

Not consumed but refreshed and at peace with the world despite all that is being said in the news, as it engulfs the cries of the people, right now.

Can you hear all the good words from preachers, teachers, and ordinary people giving so much encouragement to others, some of whom they do not know personally?

Yes, death is all around us, but so many have been healed, —of course, there are babies being born too, of which we do not hear so much about.

This trouble will be receding soon, —This is one of those ebbs of life that we must venture through!

Hello Brother, Hello Sister!

One smile began our friendship, kindred spirits we have shared.

With one word, we framed some goals along the way.

Your family being a sunbeam in this lifespan, a lit candle in times of darkness.

Oh, such laughter in common, when there is so much gloom to bear.

With one step we started a journey, with prayer, petition, and supplication —With raised spirits.

With each touch and hug, showing care,

Your voices spoke wisdom; our hearts beat in sync. It made a difference!

This is for you...

The You, of We and Us

You knocked on the door to my heart,

I said, "Who are you and Why are you here?

Tell me something good that I don't know."

You said, "This world's been kicking my behind,

Life ain't been a friend of mine,

Lately, I've been feeling kinda low."

You looked back over your shoulder,

"Do you want to take a ride with me?"

With a nod of the head, I answered, "Yes I'll go".

Went. Loved. And now, Gone.

Truly missing, the All of You,

The You, of We and Us.

You Don't See What Is Seen...

Why are you sitting there counting time?

>Look at the changes in life around you.

>Yes, there is death, but there is living, too.

>Children playing in the yard with ecstatic delight.

>A new-born babe in the arms of mommy and daddy.

Hope in the eyes of the recovering addict with a changed perspective while living amid a pandemic.

The laughter of a little girl playing with her Father lifting her to the air.

A sudden burst of energy from the widow who is still grieving as she begins to accept her loss at last.

The couple who has time to experience each other's company —not being sick, living to see a new day full of clarity for their future.

No Panic or fear by essential workers who have a love for their neighbors.

Revival, no defeat!

Gladness, no gloom!

Zeal, no apathy!

Live in this moment, for it will never be again.

We will not be the same, yet we will remember, without so much pain in the finale.

Look! See! And, Live!

In the Meantime

Smile, because of who holds tomorrow.

Smile, because without a doubt everything is going to be alright.

Smile, for overcoming the hurdles in life.

Smile, because the future will be bright,

Smile, because the past cannot dismay anymore.

Smile, and press onward.

Sunrise Over the Moon

Looked up from a good sleep-rest in my car,

To see this big sun coming up over the ocean.

Looked at it closely, as it arrived so unexpectedly,

Like a moon on fire, blazing on the face.

Oh, the warmheartedness of that sun-beaming early in the morning,

What was once seen is remembered so vividly!

So, Tiptoe unto Your Godsends

The Blessings of Waiting.

Fishing teaches us patience,

Can't rush the process, it's a lesson booster...

Sitting on the dock waiting for a bite on the angler line.

Wanting to give up with each ripple of the water.

What happens if there are no fish running in the stream?

Do you give up, and go home?

Remember, it's all in the timing.

Fishing is a slow and tedious process.

Fishing is an art. — Put in patience to succeed.

So, what is the moral of this narrative?

> Patience takes time.

> Patience takes gumption.

> Waiting is worth it; no telling what the "Creator" is up to.

Rushing may get you something that you don't need, or even want, to say the least.

Trust and Patience bring Peace to the Mind.

Uncle Alfie

You have never seen her face, only the voice you've heard.

We are family just the same. You love still.

Your calls. Your cards. They uplift each time of year and the months in between.

Love you back,   Uncle Alfie!

My Dad

A precious remembrance of you, Daddy.

I can still hear your voice, and the words you would utter each time:

"When you are coming down?" and,

"Love you, now."

"Baby Girl", you would call out.

I remember the smile on your face as you enjoyed your favorite, fried oysters.

I too, relish them today.

What was seen, I remember so tenderly.

Feeling Good

Almost time to go to the next destination of solitude.

Got a taste of what it would be like for the future.

Riding down Highway 87, turning onto Route 6!

I woke up this morning without a care in the world.

Spending time with a buddy oh my, on an overdue road trip.

Treasuring the moments is a reason for rejoicing in splendor.

Perfect Quietude.

Choose Love

Love acts,

Love matters,

Love never fails…

> Love is demonstrated in the little things we do day-by-day for our mate.
>
> Love is when you hurt inside, but choose forgiveness, instead of reprisal.
>
> Love is when you overlook the small annoyances that are bound to occur, so others can have their fun.
>
> Love is when you look at the "big picture", and can say, "it wasn't about me, anyway!"
>
> Love is laughing through the pain, so someone else can see "Agape" Love in motion.
>
> Love does not break under pressure but instead bears up, no matter what other people do.

Love is treating a person with kindness, even though you think otherwise.

Love is not gossiping, when you think you should, —to make yourself feel superior.

Love is being at peace within, letting it show in your aura.

Love is letting "the small stuff" go for the sake of serenity.

Look at the "bigger picture", choose Love...

Ascending from the Valley

When is this going to be over?

The showers. The snow. The wind keeps on knocking me down.

Need help here! N—e—e—d a pick me up!

I am crying, Calling out deep down in my soul.

Tired.

An idea popped into my mind,

Clap, Clap, Stomp, Stomp! Your way out of your broken levee.

And Count it all Joy...

Keep a Praise Inside

Remembered crying out in distress for the longest time.

One day the Master answered.

Amazed, Surprised, in Awe by the answer given.

Always said, "God has a sense of humor."

Accepted the outcome, knew it was good.

Nothing but peace on the inside, even though saddened, by it all, on the outside.

Glory, Hallelujah!

Believe.

Do not waver.

By all means, participate in the Master's process.

Greatness...

Resisting the lure of power ...

I am hearing something,

    Surrendering power.

    Serving others: absolute humbleness for the sake of love.

Turning the world upside down,

True greatness.

DELIVERER

"Delivered me from all my fears…"

Humbling moments from the beginning.

With little sustenance, less hope.

Living so disheartened,

Now see courage on the rise,

Liberated!

Opened eyes, piercing through the overcast,

Made me see, my everything to succeed.

True Love to live life

Because of You, Stronger

Not weak, no Longer

Starting journey again with all I need.

Free!

(Psalms 34:4 - "God met me more than halfway, he freed me from my anxious fears.")

One More Time

For Such A Time as This—

Thankful for this time of relaxation and fun with Loves.

This time is coming to an end shortly...

Waking up every morning with gusto in our demeanor.

Sun-setting at dusk with a gentle breeze; sunrises at dawn, so excellent!

Watching a red-tail fox looking over its back, and a turtle giving birth on the front lawn. Laughing so hard, tears start running down around the cheekbones.

Looking at the jetty on the lake. Cooking out under the big wide tent.

Quietly listening for the spirited bullfrogs to hiccup again while hiding out, disturbing the night's peace.

Neighbors dropping in to say, "Hello!"

Visiting the corner store about a mile away with all the smiles behind the counter.

Taking the trip down the million-dollar lane to the lighthouse.

Going up and down the hill on Highway 6 as it seems like you may be falling into the waters of contentment.

Laughing all the miles up the road, Oh ha! Ha! — to your next destination up the road. No traffic nowhere in sight, almost bumping into the car next to you, —now thanking the "Most High King" that you made it through.

Saying goodbye, again, to your place of tranquility on this side of paradise.

Now, it is time to do it over again!

Adjusting to the Tempests of Life

Maintaining Joy,

When suffering and troubles engulf you to the core, there is assurance amid the squalls

—The anchor of faith —the Calling on High.

When winds start to blow sideways, reach out your hands to those whirling, spiraling waves of life that so easily can knock ya down to the ground, and

Close your eyes, moan a refrain

—hummmmmmmmm —hmmmmmmmmmmm —to one of the favorite Gospel songs,

"But if the storms don't cease, And if the winds keep on blowing (in my life), My Soul has been anchored in the Lord..."

When these times of tempest arise

—Open your heart to the good around you

—Don't run from the upheaval, embrace it

Reach out to a pal who has been there, or to one who listens without any judgement.

Before you know it, you'll see that frown "turning upside down."

Voila!

Triumph comes in the morning.

The tears are dried, and the redness is gone too.

The Weather Has Nothing to Do with the Forecast

Nature is letting us know it is Springtime,

> The singing every morn and eve'ng from the neighboring trees.

> Trees blossoming,

> Bright stars in the night sky,

> Sunset after a windy, rain-falling day,

Children playing outside with such excitement as they splash in the watery puddles.

June bugs on the door glass,

A hailstorm, rainbow, and sunshine all in the same day.

Looking at people in the park, eating ice cream in their cars with the dogs hanging their heads, out of character.

> Listening to the music of the singing stream that will live in the memories.

Emphatically, No! No! —the weather has nothing to do with the forecast.

Imagine

Despair or Hope?

Obstacles come and go.

It's what you do in between the troubles of this old world that count the most.

It's hard to get out of the rut sometimes —rise above it.

You can do it!

How? Dismiss the holdbacks of that negative voice inside of you.

We all have one of those voices, you know...

Some folks can't let it go, pulling them —down —down and —down!

Look around you— There's something or someone in life's cycle that can situate you wanting to rise above it all.

But if not,

Go outside when the bees are buzzing around their most favorite nectar.

Look at the bright sunshine; Walk on the beach with the sand flowing between your toes,

Watch children playing tag. Look up at the stars at night, the moon shining brightly through the clouds.

Take a ride on a country road, and gaze at the horses galloping around the yard. Clear the mind of all the clutter gathered that had been there —almost forever!

Appreciate life's feat,

There's continuously something in this world that allows us to find the good in this, we call, "Living."

Get up, start the adventure of a lifetime!

Set the World on Fire with Your Smile

"Welfare Girl", don't feel ashamed "no more!"

Hurt and isolation, gone bye-bye.

Move your arms up and down, "Take a flight to the skies"

Never again return to the agony of what was told.

Open eyes. Open ears. Be free to love with no aching in the heart.

No more scared girl. Putting on the confidence you've been holding back so long

    —now coming into view.

May have the jitters, but not for long. This too shall pass!

Welfare Girl, you have come into your purpose; take off to your runway.

Set the world on fire with your smile.

Peace Like a Brook

Peace is likened to listening to a Brook with your eyes closed, no distraction for miles.

As you stare out across the waters running underneath the bridge, imagine your fingers gliding across the ripples, as a whisper of wind caresses your face.

No cheating now. You will miss the nautical effect.

Now, let's add the soft whistling of a gentle breeze.

Now, open your eyes gently, knowing that you have been blessed with the sheer pleasure of abundance, the overflowing triumph of a peaceful life.

Peace, like a Brook.

Happy Crying on the Inside

I cry too now

You see this smile on this face, that's the gladness in the Heart

    Oh, My!

Have you ever cried so hard that you felt an explosion inside bursting outward?

    Eyes all red,

    Eyes all puffy

Letting the gladness in!

"New Normal" Rhythm Finesse

People want to go back to work, but do we want to go back to our past "normal." Rushing here and there.

Let's be honest; most of us were stressed out of our minds. Too much stress is not good for our intellects nor physiques.

> How are you handling the "unnecessary" now that we are in "slow-down?"

Some of us are probably stressing out about the slowness of it all.

> Imagine watching the turtle crossing the "Turnpike or "Highway" during rush hour on Friday evening.

Now we are left with the "New Normal" it is too much for us to ponder as we listen to politicians, health experts, and others in the preparations for our unforeseeable future and what it will look like for us all.

This COVID-19 pandemic seems rather serious. It sneaked upon us with a vengeance. It could come back more viciously in the future. It behooves us to take our time.

> Wealth vs. Lives. Which do we value the most?

I Can, Too

Fun to pretend.

I can read,

I can love fully,

I can see beyond this realm,

I can end up being somebody in this world,

I can live life to the fullest,

I can run for President,

I can be somebody!

Why pretend?

This too is real life

    I can live free of the stigmas of this world.

Go to the Rock!

"Why, my soul, are you downcast?"

Put your hope in the "Rock of Ages",

    The "unfailing source of strength".

Why are you looking downward?

Why give into depression? Why be low, and cheerless?

    No, you're not forgotten,

The tumult of the raging seas is ceasing.

    Gladness is now increasing!

(Psalm 42:5-6)

Keep on Pushing

What comes —what may happen,

It's all up to you.

Don't look back, don't turn to either side,

The Almighty has you in this.

And by all means "Let your heart giggle!"

Going On

Resting, thinking, organizing, reminiscing, crying, and laughing out loud by myself.

Spending time with friends, family, and neighbors, wearing our masks while observing the COVID-19 distancing requirements.

Listening to raindrops, feeling sunshine on my skin, drinking a root beer float. Having a spicy chicken wing and kale - which I had last night.

Praying a lot and thanking God ceaselessly.

Taking walks around the way; watching, and hearing children outside laughing and playing hide-and-seek; go figure.

Getting through the day with my daily tasks and praying more.

I have changed again! Seeing death straight in the eye will do that for some, i.e., their way of thinking, and looking at certain things,

Life is so precious.

Looking toward the future of what God has in store for me.

That's how God is; HE never changes for me; always the same.

I am blessed. I know you are blessed too.

Keep Your Eye on the Goal

Struggles and hardships

Crushed, but not defeated

Perplexed, but not in despair

Persecuted, but not abandoned

Struck down, but not killed

Difficulties, but overcoming

Misunderstood, but not shaken

In between a rock and a hard place, but not destroyed

(2 Corinthians 4:8-9 paraphrased)

A New Thing

Some are calling this era "a new normal."

I call it "new life."

New because never done before.

For some people, this way of living right is now new

Is it new or different for you?

Our Activities are new.

Our way of doing things and situations are new.

We can't but embrace the newness of it all.

Breathing in clean air is new.

Our attitude toward this new way of life is new.

Seeing the brightest star on a clear night is new.

For some, working remotely on a full-time basis is new.

Shopping and buying options are new, especially online.

Standing in long lines to get inside the grocery store is new.

Commuting is new; hardly any traffic on the road most days —
However, people are still going fast on highways and thruways.

> Traveling is new, not many places available to travel currently.

> Interacting with each other is new; you'll have to come out of your comfort zone; otherwise, you will get lonely and isolated.

Oh, the way we talk about all of this is newness...

> Just listen to us.

The way we entertain ourselves is new.

The way we worship is new.

Videoconferencing is new for some of us. Half of us did not know it existed.

Now, this is it —newness, newness!

> The way we clean is new.

> And of course, wearing our face masks/shields and staying 6 feet apart is definitely new.

Oh, no, this is not a "new normal," this is a new way of life!

Sister Love

Looking for Love

    Understanding,

    Sister to Sister,

Love you Babygirl.

Thanks so much for sharing your wonderful testimony.

    Now I understand you.

    You were looking for family to love.

Celebrating life with you

    May God continue to bless

    In everything you do.

I love you Rae, and always will.

Snowflakes

Snowflakes falling from the "Most High's" lovely sky way up there.

Wind blowing against the trees; not a creature in sight, at this moment.

Walking slowly and thoughtfully outside,

The snowflakes hitting against my face.

Snowflakes falling from the Heavenly sky of splendor.

If I was in control

There would be no tears,

no lies,

no death,

no sleepless nights,

no anger,

no fights.

Every day would be filled

with sunshine,

with laughter in the haze,

and love all day long.

There would be

no greed,

no bad days.

Reconciliation in the world,

Everyone getting along.

Guess what, it could happen at any time now...

Skipping through Grief, with a Sniffle along the Way

The process of grieving is definitely a "downer", but if you want to be fully healed you must go through it entirely, no shortcuts here my friend.

Take all the hugs, smiles, visits, food, and desserts! Take the loving of the people encircling you, because one day it will stop completely, ultimately becoming but a murmur in the air.

You will be sitting in your lounge chair listening for the phone or doorbell to ring; or an alert that you have received a text from a friend or foe it doesn't matter! You want the distraction from the loneliness and the sheer silence of it all.

Hold up! Hold up!

Now that you are finished with the pity party ...

Let's try another approach. Let's invite some quiet living. There is nothing wrong with quietness; it makes you appreciate the noise when it comes. Quietness clears your head and gives you strength to experience a sense of thinking more clearly.

I love being around people, but I also love serenity too. Now and then give into craving the noise.

Let's be real, sometimes noise distracts so much we can't feel the pain.

Who wants to feel the pain? No one!

So, let's make it our ambition to lead a quiet life. It won't be easy, but let's have some laughs and fun along with it all and don't fully close yourself off from the world.

Hey World, coming now!

Hold On!

Time is filled with swift transitions.

So quickly, so promptly, the wink of an eye,

Nothing on this earth will stand, all things will die.

Some things are everlasting, harmony within,

Trust in God, cling close to Love from above.

Hold on when earthly folks desert,

Hold on when your money is low,

Crave not the futile riches of this world, here today and gone tomorrow.

Hope to endure the ordeal life brings.

Hold on! Hold on! Hold on!

>Lost your job —Hold On!

>Body racked with pain —-Hold On!

>Loved one has left you —Hold On!

>Nowhere to turn, but down —Hold On!

The doctor has given you a "bad report" —Hold On!

Exhausted and discouraged —Hold On!

The journey is too much. Disappointed with fear of the future —Hold On!

Build your hopes on things eternal. Keep Holding onto God's Unchanging Hand!

A-men.

Based on the Hymn by Jennie Bain Wilson

The Source

Oh, how deliberate, You were meant to go,

You are not in this Alone,

Reach out of the "safe" zone,

Someone's there to help,

Look beyond the reach.

Indescribable

Loneliness and Comfort at the same time...

I am having a moment —amid a lovely day.

I am enjoying one of the best times with my Loves – I will remember this day with fond memories while looking back with contentment.

> The music blasting from the "mini" Bluetooth speakers with Al Green and Teddy Pendergrass! I love these artists of the past.

Right now, I am watching the nearby couples as they are going about their day, eating their lunch, appreciating each other's company.

> Some of us have been out all day fishing in the sea of weeds, but only one of us caught the "big one!"

We others wished we could have done better —Lost rod wares; the worms didn't work either.

As this day ends, I am feeling so alone. What to do?

> I am thinking of a loved one of the past, missing their presence, finding the comfort of being surrounded by the reminiscences of those who loved so true.

Remember You

Can't forget that face standing at the door wanting to know my name

Kept coming back for an answer,

"Are you here again?"

"Yes or no?" —the queries.

Say yes, you are different!

> What is it about you that makes me want to endeavor to be in love again?

Finally, worn down.

Give up!

You got me, right in the heart,

Said yes...

A Million in One

Some say sagacious; some say courageous, some have said, "you can do it,

Don't be afraid."

Some say, you are kind; some say you are the MVP!

Some say, you are so positive and inspiring,

Some say, you are devoted, attentive, enthusiastic, and confident.

Some say, what a gem.

Some call you friend, and some even enemy, but you are loved the same.

Some call you amazing, some say you are wise.

You are appreciated.

You are loved.

At the end of the day.

I am Me.

Uncertain Future

This is a difficult time, need guidance.

Hopes, dreams, preparations, expectations put on hold.

Right now, feeling like a sailor, contemplating whether to set sail or not.

The future is uncertain and veiled from sight.

There's a plan already mapped out for all of us, even though it may be hidden for a season.

Adjust your sails...

Living Proof of Inner Strength

There are times in our lives when we must spread our wings like a caterpillar becoming a butterfly.

Stop struggling. Go through those times of change, no matter how difficult it becomes.

As with the butterfly, life goes on, can't go back no matter how hard it tries.

In the same way, once you pass through your struggles, you will be changed forever.

You're never going back.

Reflecting upon past and present —wouldn't change a thing.

Today, starting a brand-new aspect of living, Alone!

There are a lot of things to be done yet.

Yesterday was good. Tomorrow will lead. The future is in front and center.

Why so much pain? Won't complain—the living proof.

"Butterflies can't see their wings. They can't see how beautiful they are, but everyone else can. People are like that."
- Naya Rivera

Reflections: RCA's Praise Song

No more fear,

    In Almighty One's hands.

No more tears,

    Moving on to the next millennium.

You have been carried thus far, throughout this lifespan.

Looking forward to more happiness!

Goodbye sorrow and pain,

    Free to live in the present.

No loudness, but calm,

Gladness and amusement within,

Sitting here rejoicing in this most precious time.

Oh, what liberty!

Nothing Moves until You Speak!

Say it Loud!

    No more silence in the air.

Speak up!

    Without repercussions.

Because it's the right time to make a change in these words of ours.

What do we have to lose?

This time of slow-down is a momentous time for transformation,

    Find your way through it all.

    Don't misunderstand, don't be foolish.

    Be reasonable with your thoughts,

Speak up, speak out and share your voice,

    The world is counting on it!

Tenacity

No quitting,

    Moving forward,

Goal-setting stubborn to the bone.

Taking a grip on the world,

Holding on,

    Never giving up.

Marching and taking the world by surprise,

    With the spiritual fervor within.

It's Up to You

Sing a song for the moment,

Start a conversation to frame an agreement.

Pick a flower to start the dream,

Of a friendship beam.

Sit under a tree in the forest,

Listen for a song chorus.

Clasp a hand to lift a soul,

Let out a gigantic laugh to conquer the gloomy role.

Vote to change a nation,

It will be good for our global relations.

Let in some sunshine in the room.

Light a candle to wipe out the gloom.

Take that first step toward your journey.

Reach out and touch someone to raise their spirits,

That One touch can show you care.

THOU!

Thank you, for all Thou hast done —great things

Thou made way when there was no way in or out

    Living in victory,

    Giving Thou the Praise!

Thank you for a new life – It was Thou who stepped in and saved me,

    Down-and-out, Thou raised me up —Thank You!

    Brought me through tribulations —Thank You!

    Kept me in the "land of the living" —Thank You!

When mind snapped, Thou renewed my mindset —Thank You!

Homeless, Thou lifted me out of the "gutter most" —Thank You!

All alone, Thou was a Friend —Thank you!

    This thankful heart goes out to Thee.

    It was Thou, Creator, and Sustainer —Thank You.

"Thou art the Rock that arms with strength, that makes life on this earth perfect.

It is Thee, who makes these feet like the feet of deer —And Sets me on my high places". (Psalm 18:32, 33 NIV, paraphrased).

Family Friends

Spending time together.

Sharing a meal and a chuckle or two.

Not blood, but kindred spirits which come from above.

You were there all along.

Love is unconditional.

Forever, until we depart this earth.

You Can Make It

No matter how you feel inside right now …

Soul's broken.

Hungry, no job,

Been harshly mistreated,

Loss of a baby early in the process,

No friends in sight, kinfolk absent.

No heat in the house, rats running rampant.

Bills piling up, eating apples, eating hot chili every day,
with a burning tongue.

In the food line, no hope in sight,

Cannot get food stamps, make too much.

Felt ashamed to tell the story.

It's not over; Hope is on the rise for you.

Look to the "Bigger One".

Things to Live With

How do you feel about your life today?

Are you living every day with excitement?

Do you love what you're doing?

Are you looking forward to what's coming next?

Are you living your best life?

>Holding yourself to the highest conduct.

>Letting go of an unhappy past.

>Forgiving those who have done you wrong.

>Practicing gratitude.

>Loving others.

Be grateful for all the people around you because they help you grow.

"Your time is limited, don't waste it living someone else's life. Don't be trapped by dogma, which is living the result of other people's thinking. Don't let the noise of other's opinion drown your own inner voice. And most important, have the courage to follow your heart and intuition, they somehow already know what you truly want to become. Everything else is secondary." –<u>Steve Jobs</u>

Wrong Focus = Frustration

Wrong Focus equals frustration

Stop trying to do what others do.

Imitating another's life is not the way to go forward.

What frustrates you?

Hoopla? Gossiping? Hate?

Remain focused on the outcomes, not the obstacles.

Joy in the Morning

Finding Hope midst of the struggle.

Dark nights, hours of fear, moments of uncertainty, anxiety,

There is a plan that is ultimately good for you.

"May God bless you and keep you in your darkest night and moments of greatest fear and uncertainty. May you see His face in every moment today and find hope in the promise of a most beautiful dawn that is already on its way - a morning filled with joy. Amen![1]

"For I know the plans I have for you," declares the Lord, *"plans to prosper you and not to harm you, plans to give you hope and a future."* (Jeremiah 29:11, New International Version)

---

1 Source: https://www.crosswalk.com/faith/bible-study/joy-comes-in-the-morning-how-psalm-305-celebrates-resurrection.html

RESILIENCE

It is said "Tough times never last", that

"Scars remind us where we've been," and that

"You never know how strong you are, until being strong is your only choice."

It is said, "It's hard to beat a person who never gives up."

In the Stillness of the Day

Looking at dewdrops, so comforting to the mind.

It's quiet, almost feel a nap coming right about now.

Oh, how excellent it is to practice patient attention to your serene surroundings.

Hearing the wind and feeling the cool breeze coming through the cracks in the screened door.

Feeling free…

The tree branches are dancing in the wind.

> Look at them sashaying.

Look at the "flowering pear" tree tearing up from the beauty of the daytime,

> Their white buds drop all over the place; and blowing to and fro as if to say,

> "I be joyful"!

Oh, how comforting to be wrapped in the tranquil stillness.

What If?

Yesterday, today...

Where do you start?

Picking yourself up.

Thanking the Master for the strength to go on.

Looking deep inside,

>Wasn't expecting this loss so soon.

Taking inventory of your life.

>Looking to make things right,

>Tired of the old ways.

What if you fail?

>"Sometimes, being strong means not holding back the tears but letting them fall."

Hearing this whisper in your ear.

>You can do it!

Walking into your destiny.

The Circus

The Soul Circus

Full of elephants, chimps, and dancing dogs.

I felt like a kid a minute ago.

Muscle-bound men on stilts stepping to calypso strutting across the sandy floor.

Zak, the small miniature person, making us burst with laughter,

And not to forget Casual Cal the Ringmaster.

Oh! Those magnificent acrobat acts!

What a day at the circus we had today.

Keep in Step with the Spirit

Do you hear it!?

    An utterance, low and sacred.

    It's softer than a whisper.

Can you hear it?

    The fluttering hummingbird's wing in slow motion —
    cheery and precise.

Can you see it?

    It's like watching someone's chest rising and lowering
    as they

        —inhale   —exhale

    Slowly   —in -and   —out, without much effort.

Then again, it's like a wispy wind blowing through the trees,
the soothing sound of the rain with it.

Can you hear it?

ACKNOWLEDGEMENTS

For my friends and family who have walked every step of this journey with me, thank you. Your love gave me the strength and the hope to continue forward when I had neither. Thank you for loving me as I am...

For my Joy Missionary Baptist Church Family, thank you for your welcoming, encouraging, and loving spirit toward me. Pastor Campbell and First Lady Annie, thank you for your love toward me from the very start of this new journey not so long ago.

To the Messiah Baptist Church members, thank you for your good wishes in this endeavor of mine.

Thank you, the Lincoln Ministries family, and friends, for remembering me and for the hugs each time I am in your presence.

To my Tri-County Talkers Toastmasters International associates, thank you so much for your guidance, encouragement, and assessment at each time I spoke before you.

For my colleagues at the "WIB" and "CC," of which many have known me for many years, thank you for making me feel so special through my moments of grandeur.

To my writing Coach, the Rev. Dr. Kirk Byron Jones, "Mr. Power-Up," you were a Godsend at the right time. Your encouragement, support, and commendation have been a tremendous joy for me.

I would be remiss if I did not send out a big shout-out to two of my favorite Pastors, both of whom have poured into me spiritually with your preaching and teachings for a span of more than 20 years. Thank you both, the Rev. Huston Crayton, Jr., and the Rev. Dr. Michael W. Walker.

To my FIRST RESPONDERS, my manuscript pages reviewers, Lena Rose, Jewell Wilson, Delores Hudgins, Jeanette Dalton, Shaleah Gilmer, The Rev. Samuel L. Campbell, Sr. and Rev. Dr. Kirk Byron Jones, your contributions of candid feedback, and your skills of checking, and rechecking as you proofed the total manuscript for unintentional repetitions, clichés, and other redundancies. Your encouragement kept me going. Thank you for your precious gifts of time, patience, and honesty.

It is needless to add, but I do so nevertheless, that the responsibility for the final form and content of these pages is mine, with the help of the "Superintendent of my Life's Railway."

In Memoriam

Thomas Adams

Beloved husband, friend,

and confidant

Whose life inspired

PART 2 COMING SOON